PSYCHOLOGIST
COLORING BOOK

THIS BOOK BELONGS TO:

____

I'M A
Psychologist
NOT A
Magician

I'M A
PSYCHOLOGIST
WHAT'S YOUR
SUPER
POWER?

Relax
WE'RE ALL
CRAZY!
IT'S NOT A
COMPETITION

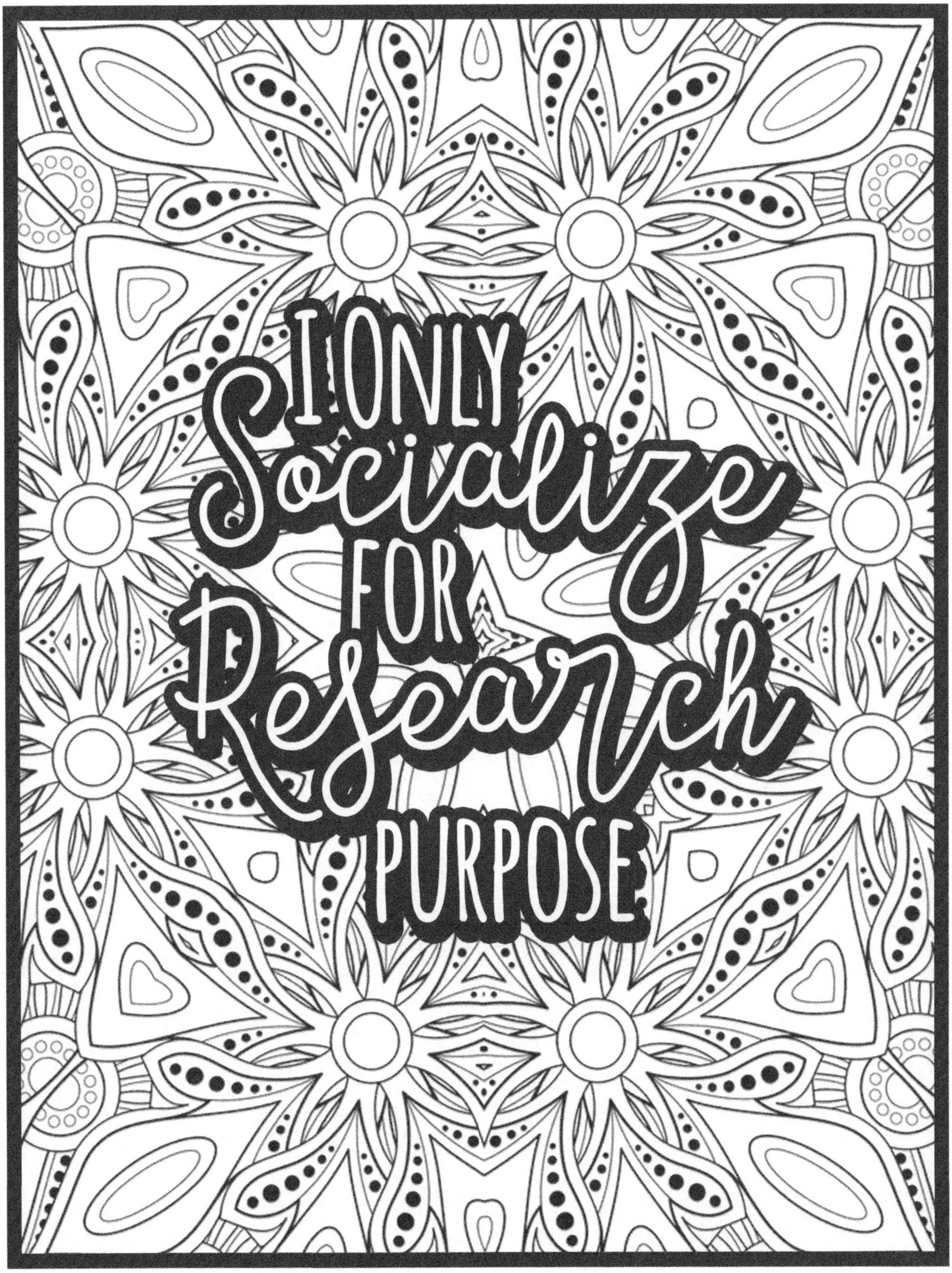
I ONLY
Socialize
FOR
Research
PURPOSE

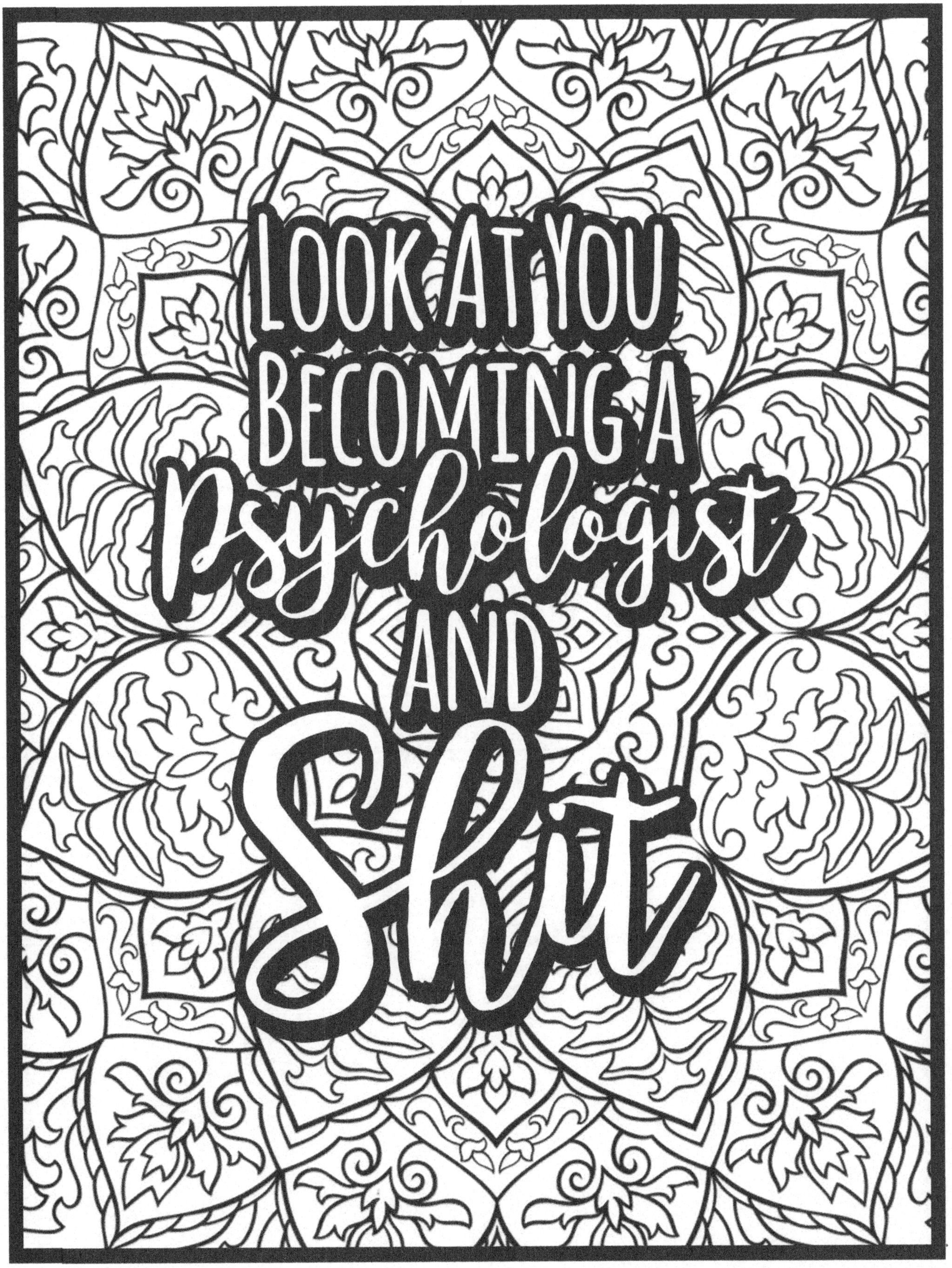
LOOK AT YOU
BECOMING A
Psychologist
AND
Shit

I'm
Afreud
to
Love!

KEEP TALKING
I'M
Diagnosing
You

World's
BEST
Psychologist

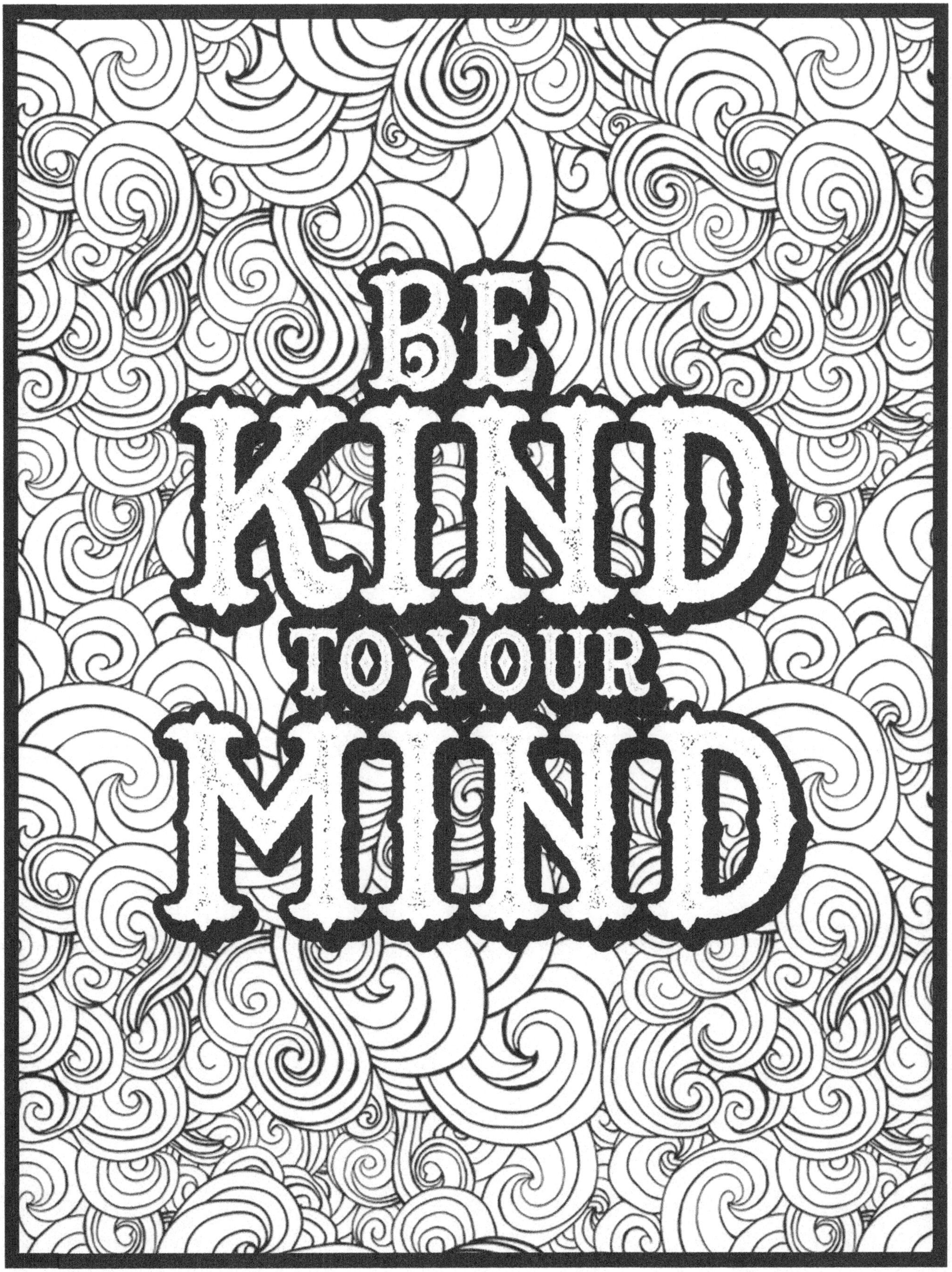
BE
KIND
TO YOUR
MIND

Because
i'm the
psychologist
That's Why!

One Patient
away
From
Becoming a
patient

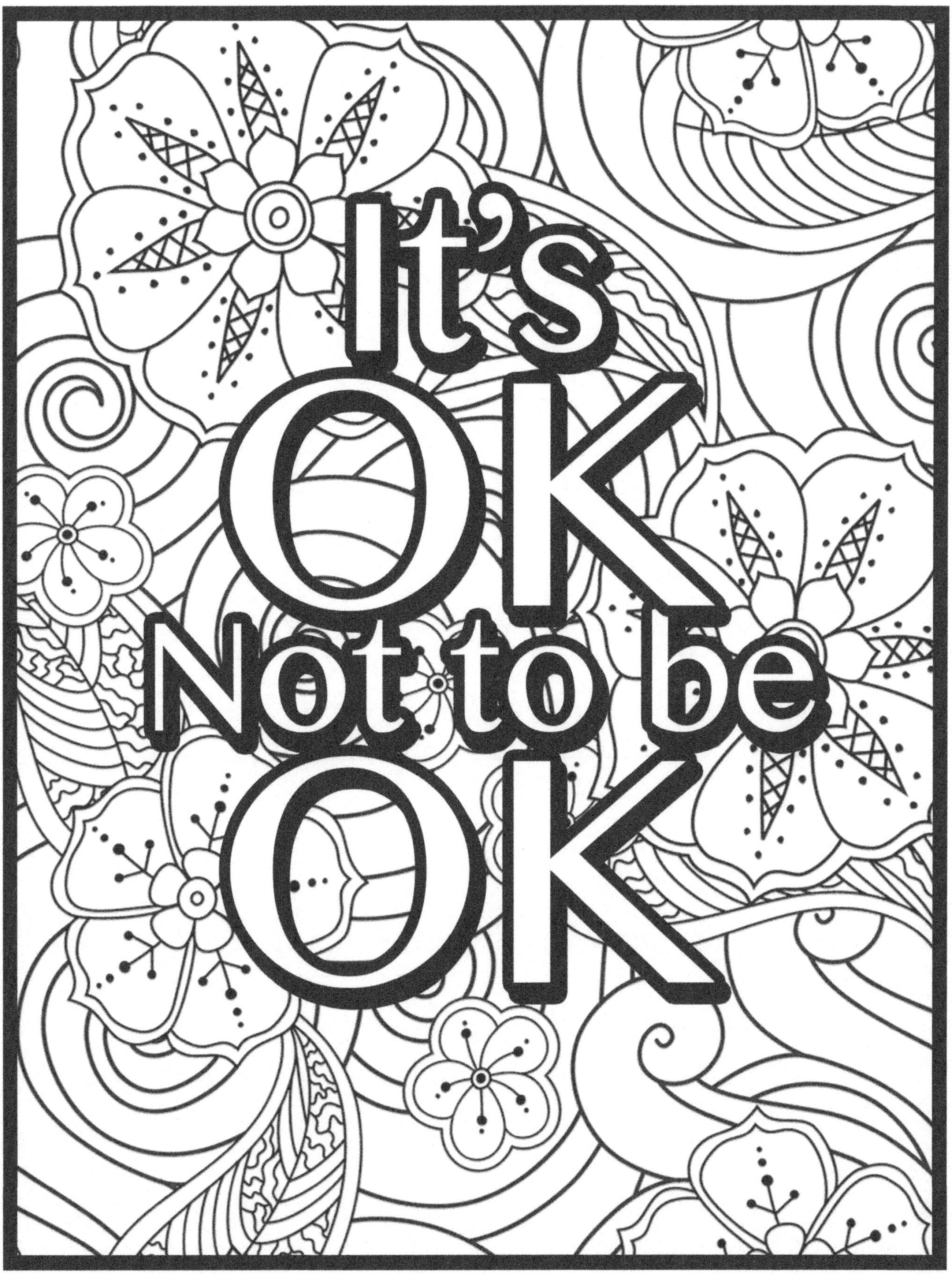
It's
OK
Not to be
OK

DON'T MAKE
ME USE MY
Psychologist
VOICE

I Chose
the
Psycho
Path

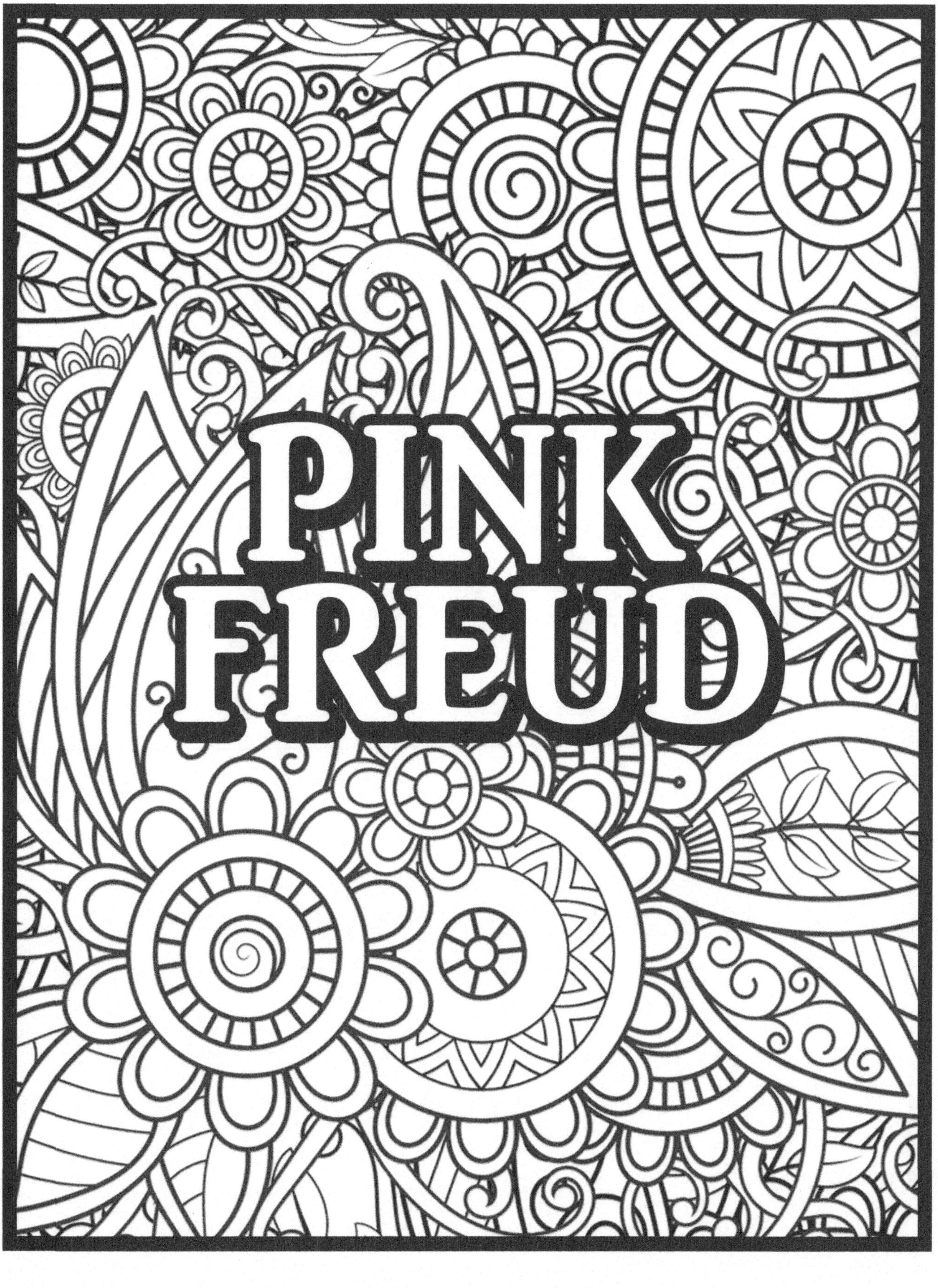
PINK
FREUD

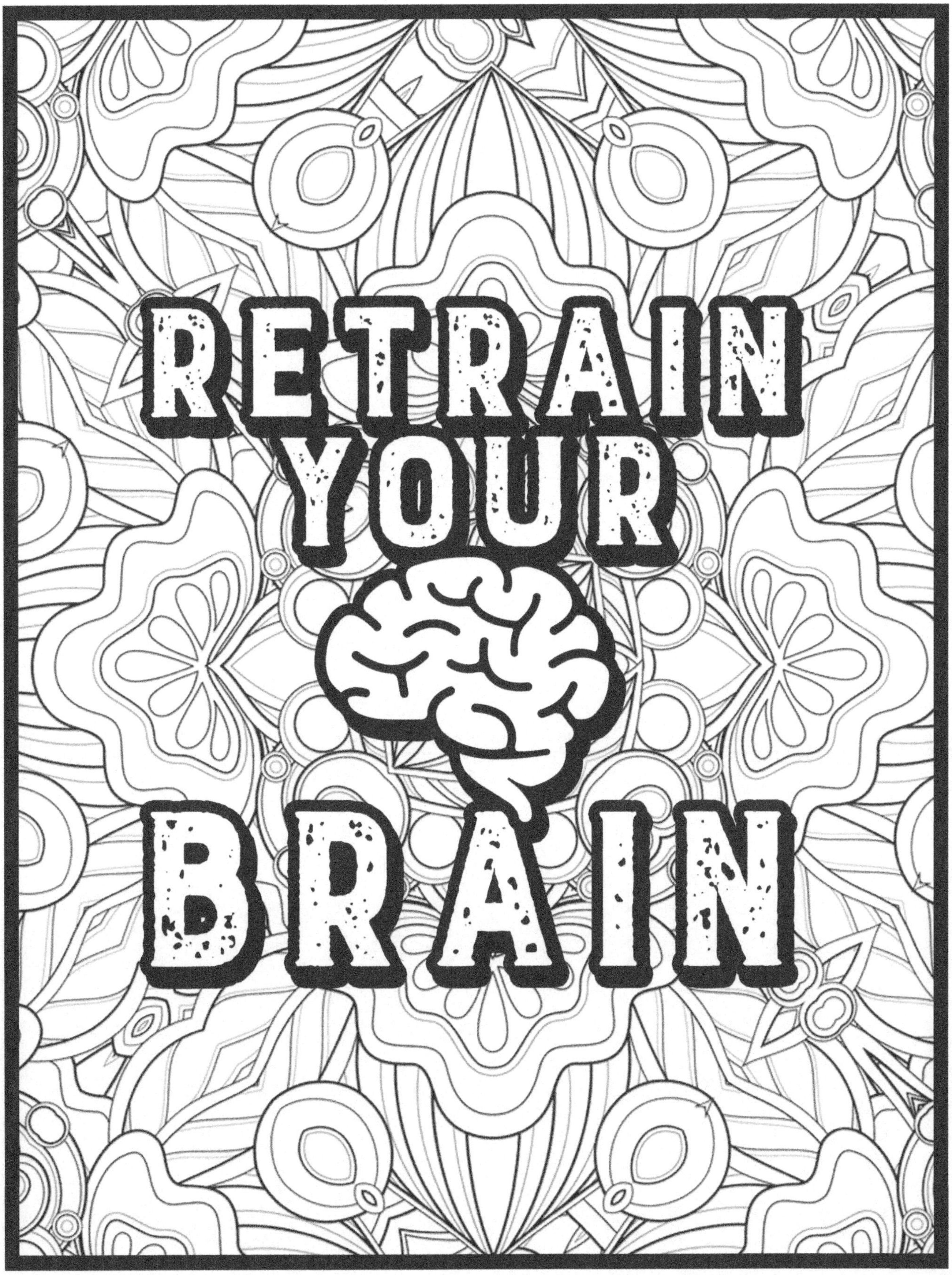
RETRAIN YOUR
BRAIN

PSYCHOLOGY
I'M
ALLERGIC
TO STUPIDITY
I BREAK OUT IN
Sarcasm

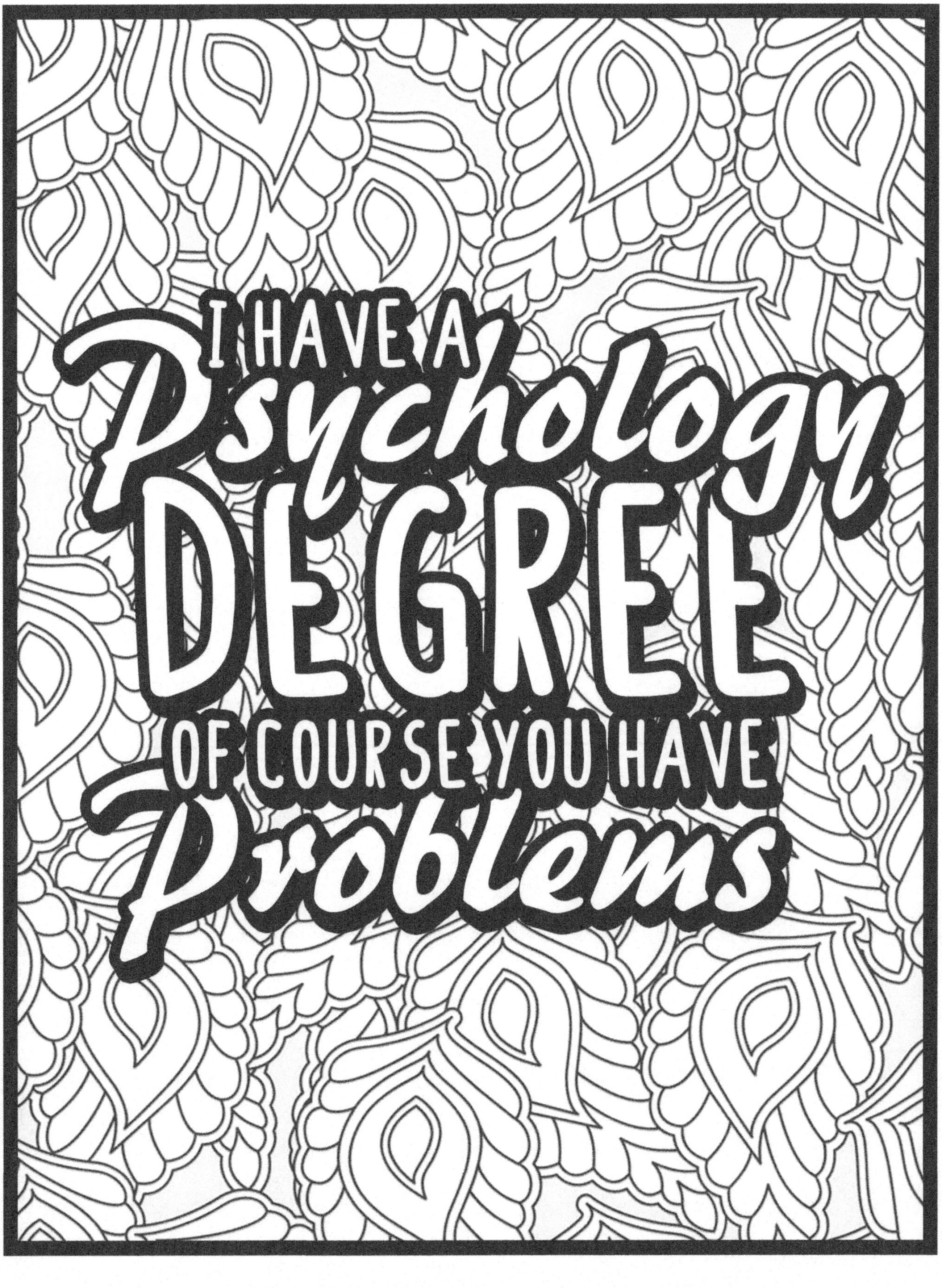
I HAVE A
Psychology
DEGREE
OF COURSE YOU HAVE
Problems

THIS
Psychologist
NEEDS A
MOTHER
FUCKING
Nap!

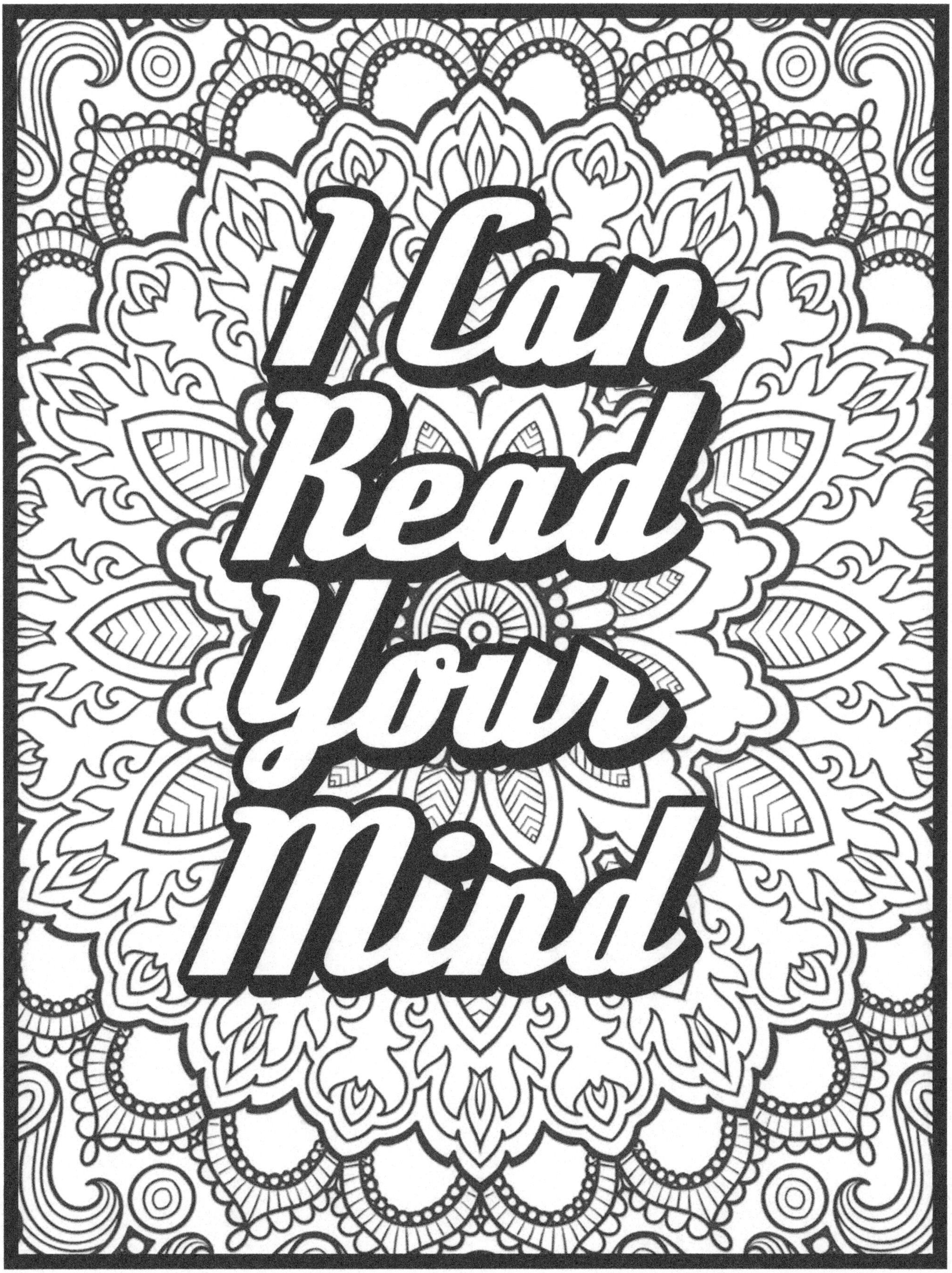
I Can
Read
Your
Mind

Made in the USA
Monee, IL
03 November 2021

81381922R00024